ADDISON-WESLEY
ESL

Michael Walker

Original Music by Bob Schneider

Addison-Wesley Publishing Company

Reading, Massachusetts • Menlo Park, California • New York • Don Mills, Ontario • Wokingham, England
Amsterdam • Bonn • Sydney • Singapore • Tokyo • Madrid • San Juan

Contents

─────── **A Publication of the World Language Division** ───────

Editor-in-Chief: Judith Bittinger
Project Director: Elinor Chamas
Editorial Development: Elly Schottman, Talbot Hamlin
Production/Manufacturing: James W. Gibbons
Rights Coordination: Merle Sciacca
Design, Art Direction, and Production: Taurins Design Associates, New York
Cover Art: Laurie Jordan
Illustrators: Teresa Anderko 16, 17, 35, 38, 97; Ellen Appleby 5, 90; Susan Avishai 49, 72, 73, 107, 114, 115; Don Baker 13, 43, 87; Karen Bell 46, 108, 110; Lee Lee Brazeal 78, 99, 100, 101, 102, 103, 104; Jane Chambless 39, 40, 41, 42; Chi Chung 59, 60, 61, 62; Maryann Cocca 8, 48, 76, 77, 112; Nancy Didion 14, 15, 36, 37, 113; Design Five 4, 10; David Frampton 19, 20, 21, 22; Annie Gusman 58, 98; Ann Iosa 30, 34, 68. 85, 109, 111; Laurie Jordan 79, 80, 81, 82; Elliot

Kreloff 33; Bruce Lemerise 34; Susan Lexa 3, 9, 26, 27, 54, 55, 64, 66, 70, 94, 95, 105, 106; Karen Loccisano 6, 7, 11, 31, 44, 45, 50, 51, 71, 74, 91, 116, 117; Karen Merbaum 119; Cyd Moore 120; Diane Palmisiano 24, 32, 52, 92; Debbie Pinkney 12, 18, 25, 47, 83, 118; Jerry Smath 23, 63; Joel Snyder 7, 44; John Wallner 28, 29, 89; Ulises Wensell 121-127; Jane Yamada 65, 67, 84, 86, 88.
Photographers: G.V. Faint, The Image Bank bottom left 56; Mark E. Gibson, The Stock Market top right 56; Larry Dale Gordon bottom right 56; Judy Gurovitz 16, 17, 37, 87, 96; Doug Handel, The Stock Market 97; Ann Heimann, The Stock Market bottom right 57; Michal Heron, Woodfin Camp & Associates bottom left 57; J.T. Miller, The Stock Market top left 57; Gabe Palmer, The Stock Market top right 57; R. Semeniuk, The Stock Market middle left 57; J.L. Stage, The Image Bank, top left 56.

Acknowledgments: Page 18, "This Land Is Your Land," Words and music by Woody Guthrie, TRO — © Copyright 1956 (renewed 1984), 1958 and 1970 Ludlow Music, Inc. New York, New York. All rights reserved including public performance for profit. Used by permission. Pages 39-42, Adapted from *Bambi*, by Felix Salten, copyright © 1928 by Simon & Schuster, Inc. Translated by Whittaker Chambers. Reprinted by permission of Simon & Schuster, Inc., Jonathan Cape Ltd, and the executors of the Felix Salton estate. Page 120, "Dreams," from *The Dream Keeper and Other Poems*, by Langston Hughes. Copyright 1932 by Alfred A. Knopf, Inc. and renewed 1960 by Langston Hughes. Reprinted by permission of Alfred A. Knopf, Inc.

ISBN 0-201-57816-6
7 8 9 10 11 12-DA-98 97 96 95

At School

1. table
2. chair
3. door
4. desk
5. clock
6. window
7. wall
8. chalkboard
9. bookcase

Identifying classroom items
TPR

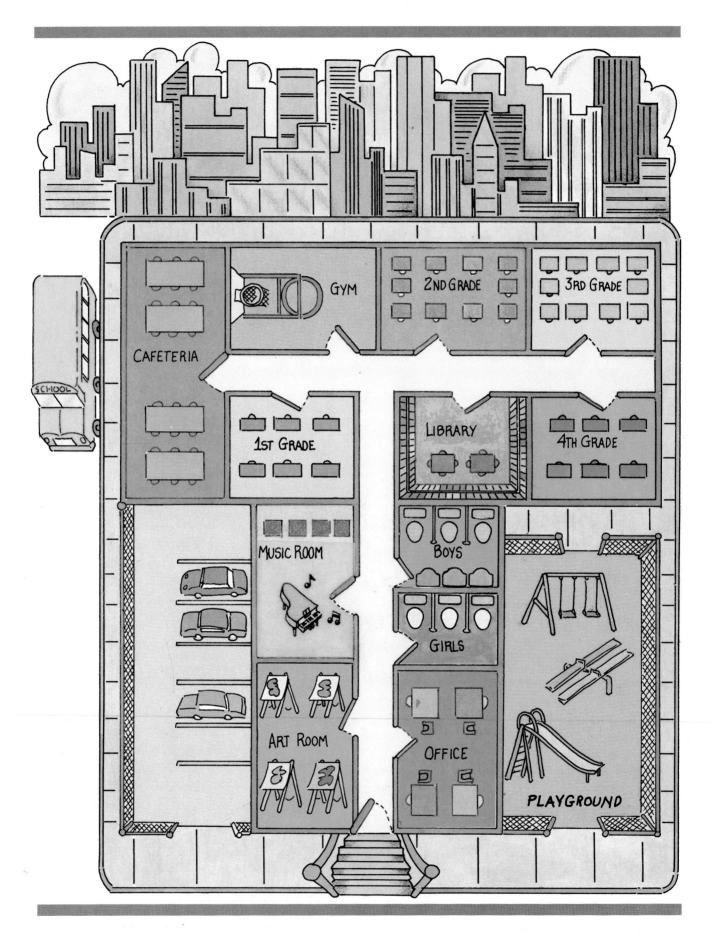

Identifying places in school
Asking for/giving directions

The Alphabet Cheer

Give me an A!
Give me a B!
Give me an ABCDEFG!
Give me an H!
Give me an I!
Give me an HIJKLMNOP!
Give me a Q!
Give me an R!
Give me a QRSTUVW!
Give me an X!
Give me a Y!
Give me a Z!
So tell me now,
What did you get?

A!
B!
ABCDEFG!
H!
I!
HIJKLMNOP!
Q!
R!
QRSTUVW!
X!
Y!
Z!
I think we got
The alphabet!

Music: identifying letters
Reciting the alphabet in order

Asking for/giving personal information
Role-playing fixed and free dialogues

Do you like **animals?**

Yes, I do.

No, I don't.

1. movies

2. vegetables

3. books

4. games

5. ice cream

6. fruit

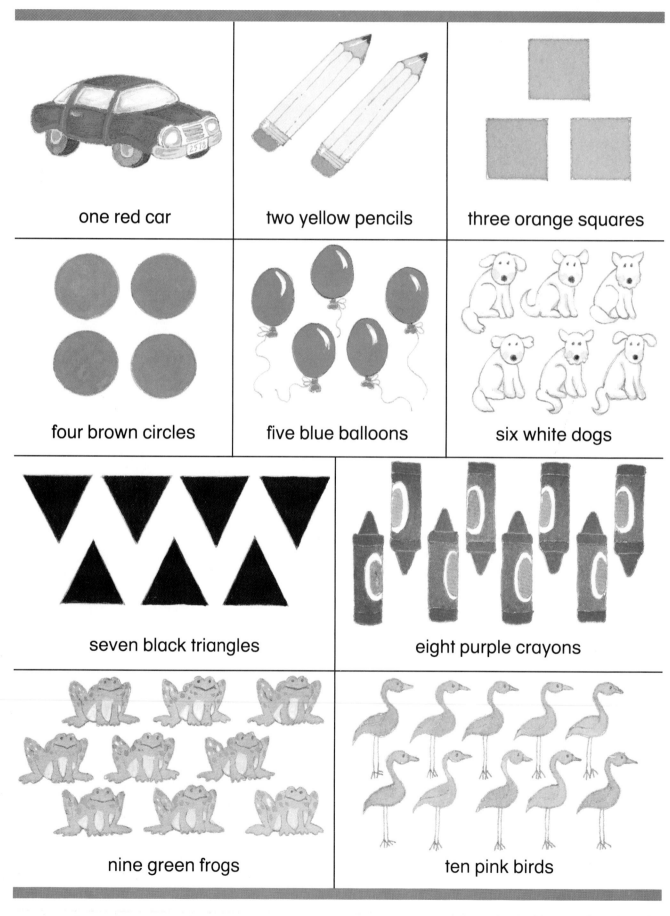

one red car

two yellow pencils

three orange squares

four brown circles

five blue balloons

six white dogs

seven black triangles

eight purple crayons

nine green frogs

ten pink birds

Counting to 10
Identifying colors/number words

1. dance

2. draw

3. swim

4. skate

5. run

6. read

 Asking for/giving personal information
Role-playing fixed and free dialogues
Music: creating original verses

9

Identifying months/holidays
Asking for/giving personal information

Pair Practice

What's your name?

My name is Dorothy Chin.

What's the name of your school?

I go to Cosby School.

What's your address?

My address is 416 Green Street, Los Angeles, California.

What's your phone number?

My phone number is 465-2139.

Make conversations about these people.

1.
Mario Perry
Lake Street School
19 West Avenue
New York City, New York
751-0348

2.
Sally White
John Reagan School
82 River Road
Dallas, Texas
553-6794

Now talk about yourself with a partner.

Role-playing fixed and free dialogues
Creating new dialogues from cues
Talking about self

11

Listening Comprehension

Listen carefully. Choose the best picture.

Listening Progress Check
Matching spoken language to pictures

Reading Comprehension

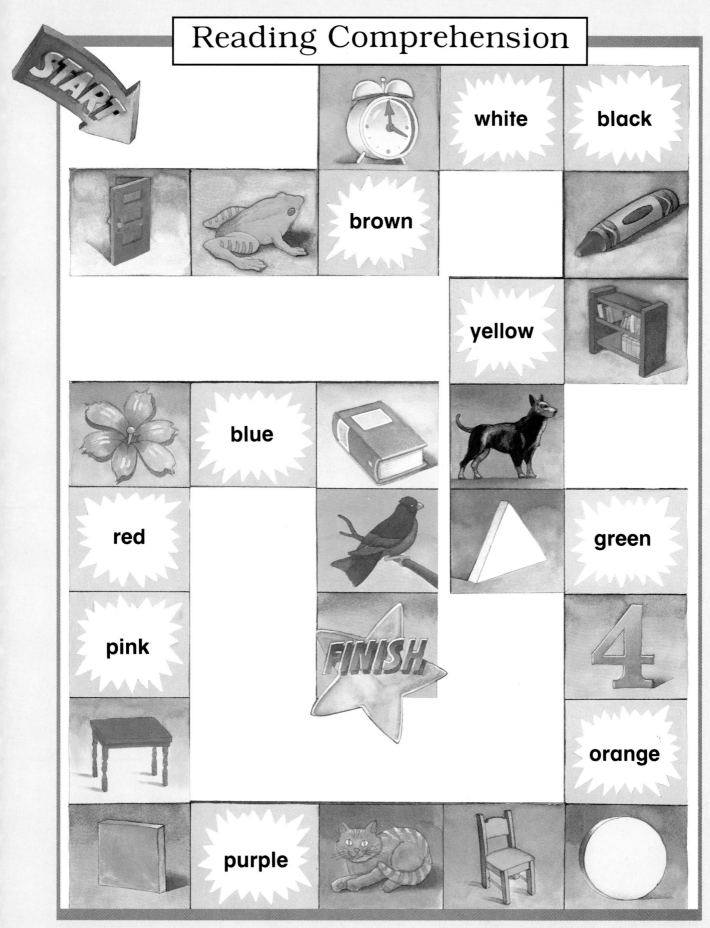

Reading Progress Check
Game: identifying colors and objects
Socializing/turn-taking

13

Say the right thing!

Happy birthday!
It's my birthday today.

Thank you.
I know. How old are you?

I'm twelve.
Here's a present.

Oh, what is it?
I hope you like this present.

Open it and find out.
Oh, a new game. Thank you.

A red T-shirt! Thanks a lot!
You're welcome.

Do you want to play it?
I know you like red.

Sure.
Yes, red is my favorite color.

Make conversations with your partner.
Begin with these situations.

1. It's your birthday.
   You're ten.
   You get a red hat.
   Red is your favorite color.

2. It's your sister's birthday.
   She's eighteen.
   You give her a blue T-shirt.
   Blue is her favorite color.

Role-playing fixed dialogues
Following conversation sequence
Creating new dialogues from cues

15

Measuring

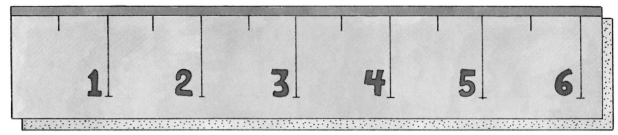

The marks on this ruler show inches.
There are 12 inches in a foot.

Use a ruler.
How long is your pencil?

How wide is your desk?

Measure around your wrist.
Cut the string.
A friend can help you.

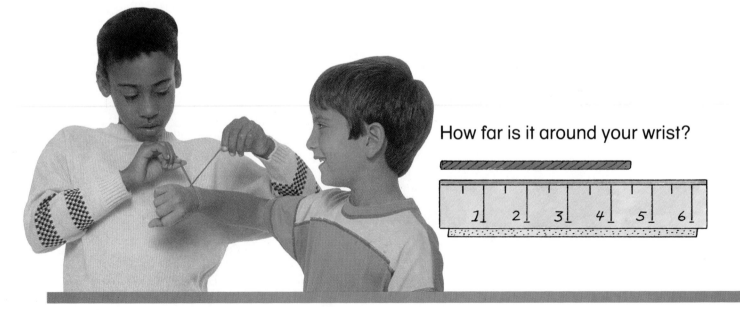

How far is it around your wrist?

Make a scale.

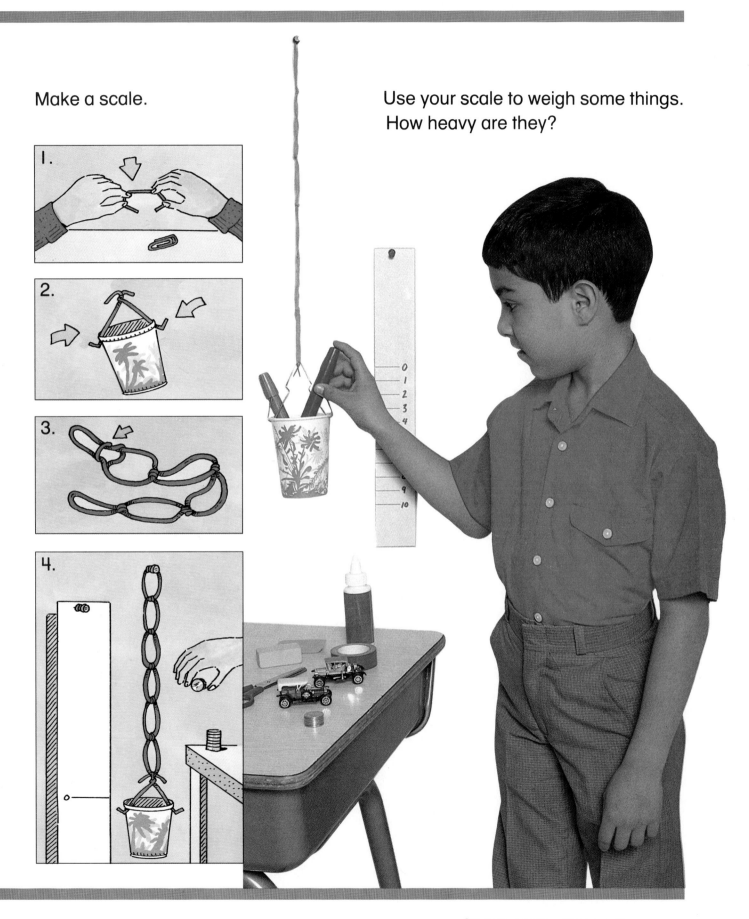

1.

2.

3.

4.

Use your scale to weigh some things.
How heavy are they?

0
1
2
3
4

9
10

This Land Is Your Land

Words and music by Woody Guthrie

This land is your land,
This land is my land,
From California,
To the New York island;
From the redwood forest,
To the Gulf Stream waters;
This land was made for you and me.

Music: folk song
Social studies: U.S. geography
Creative writing

Columbus

Christopher Columbus lived in Genoa, Italy. He was a sailor. He sailed on many ships to many places. He wanted to sail to Asia. In those days, people called Asia "The Indies." They traveled east to get there. They went across land and water. The trip was long and very dangerous.

Columbus had a different idea. He wanted to sail *west!* Many people said, "That's crazy. The world is flat. You'll sail off the edge of the world. You'll never come back." Columbus didn't listen. He was sure the world was round.

The King and Queen of Spain gave Columbus money and three ships.

Literature: historical non-fiction

In 1492, Columbus sailed west. His ships were the Niña, the Pinta, and the Santa Maria. After a month at sea, the men wanted to turn back. Columbus didn't listen. "Sail on," he said. After two months, Columbus saw land.

Columbus thought he was on an island in the Indies. He called the people there "Indians." He thought he had discovered a new route to Asia. But he had discovered something much more important. He had discovered a new world!

Literature: historical non-fiction

At Home

1. kitchen	4. living room	7. bathroom
2. refrigerator	5. couch	8. tub
3. stove	6. bedroom	9. sink

★ What's she wearing?
● She's wearing a **blue blouse.**

   1. blouse
   2. sweater
   3. skirt
   4. hat

★ What's he wearing?
● He's wearing **green pants.**

   1. pants
   2. shoes
   3. socks
   4. gloves

★ What are they wearing?
● They're wearing **blue jackets.**

   1. jackets
   2. jeans
   3. sneakers
   4. glasses

Describing colors/clothes
Asking for/giving information
Role-playing fixed and free dialogues; Music

★ What are they eating?
● They're eating **cereal and bananas**.

1. rice
2. fish
3. meat
4. soup
5. eggs
6. beans
7. apples
8. sandwiches
9. oranges
10. peaches
11. ice cream
12. cheese

Asking for/giving information
Identifying foods
Role-playing fixed and free dialogues

25

This is Tom's family.
His father is tall and thin.
His mother is short and pretty.
His sister is chubby.
Tom is just average.

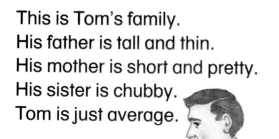

This is Kim's family.
Her mother is tall.
Her grandmother is short.
Her brother is thin.
Kim is tall and pretty.

What about Tom's uncle?

What about Kim's aunt?

Describing family members
Using kinship terms
Personal story-telling

How many brothers does she have?　　She has two brothers.

How many sisters does she have?　　She has one sister.

Does she have a pet?　　Yes, she has a bird.

How many aunts does he have?　　He has three aunts.

How many cousins does he have?　　He has four cousins.

Does he have a pet?　　Yes, he has a hamster.

Identifying possessions

He is hiding. But I can see him.
She is hiding. But I can see her.

You are hiding. But I can see you.
They are hiding. But I can see them.

I am hiding. Can you see me?
We are hiding. Can you see us?

behind   in front of   next to   under   on   in

Describing location
Music: folk song

Pair Practice

Is your family big or small?

My family is big.

How many brothers do you have?

I have two brothers.

What are their names?

Dan and Mike.

How many sisters do you have?

I have three sisters.

What are their names?

Susan, Judy, and Ellen.

Do you have a pet?

No, I don't. But I'd like a hamster for my birthday.

Make conversations about these families.

1.

2.

Now talk about your family.

Role-playing fixed and free dialogues
Creating new dialogues from cues
Talking about self

31

Listening Comprehension

Listen carefully. Choose the best picture.

Listening Progress Check
Matching spoken language to pictures

Reading Comprehension

Reading Progress Check
Game: prepositions/nouns
Socializing/turn-taking

33

I need a spoon.

Pass the butter, please.

More chicken?

Yes, please.

May I have some more carrots?

DATA BANK

pepper

sugar

bread

salt

spaghetti

salad

fruit

pizza

fork

knife

napkin

glass

Say the right thing!

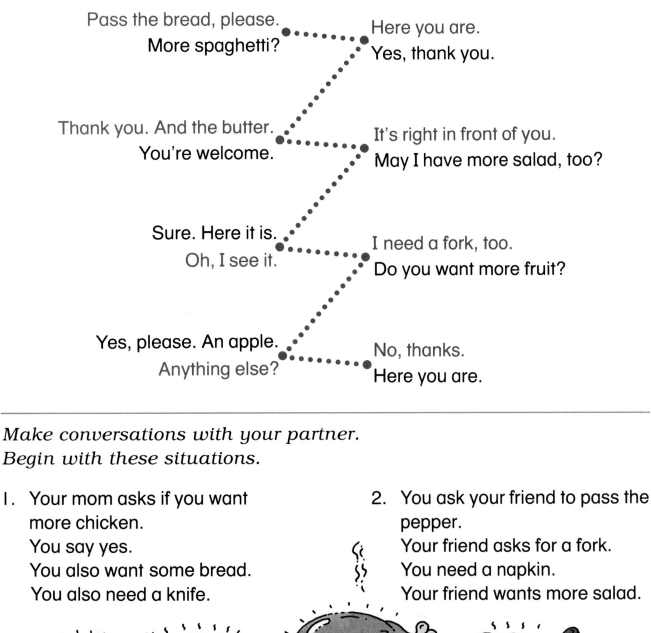

Pass the bread, please. ⟶ Here you are.
More spaghetti? Yes, thank you.

Thank you. And the butter. It's right in front of you.
You're welcome. May I have more salad, too?

Sure. Here it is. I need a fork, too.
Oh, I see it. Do you want more fruit?

Yes, please. An apple. No, thanks.
Anything else? Here you are.

Make conversations with your partner.
Begin with these situations.

1. Your mom asks if you want more chicken.
   You say yes.
   You also want some bread.
   You also need a knife.

2. You ask your friend to pass the pepper.
   Your friend asks for a fork.
   You need a napkin.
   Your friend wants more salad.

Role-playing fixed dialogues
Understanding sequence in conversations
Creating new dialogues from cues

35

Your Bones

This picture shows the bones in your body.
You have three bones in each leg.
Feel the top bone in your leg.
This is the longest bone in your body.

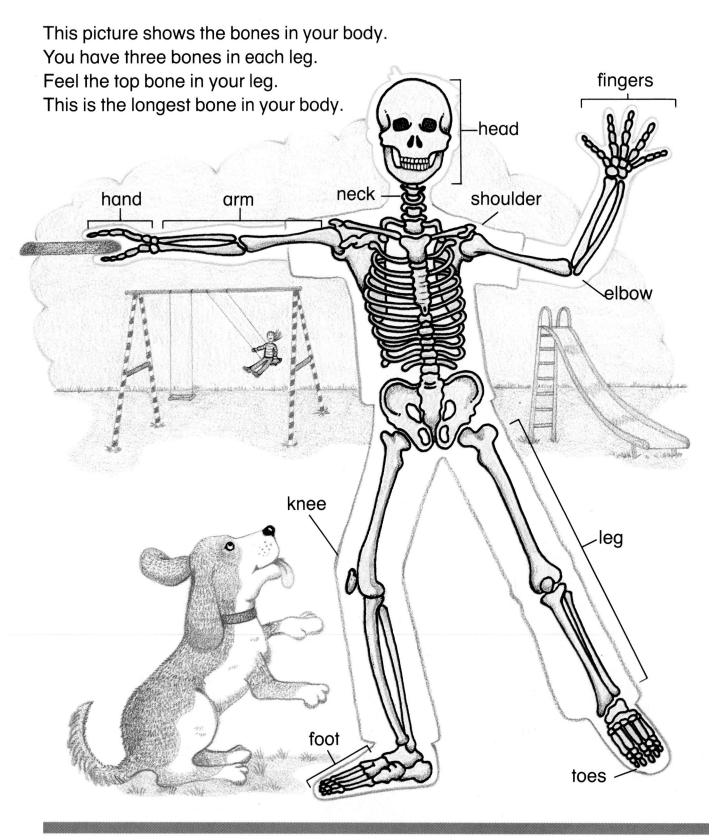

CALLA: Imagery

Your Heart

Your heart is a muscle.
Your heart beats all day and all night.
When you move, your heart beats faster.

heart

Put your fingers on your neck.
Count your heartbeats for half a minute.
Now jump 30 times.
Count your heartbeats again.

The Salt and Pepper Shake

Music: TPR
Identifying body parts
Creative writing

Bambi

Adapted from the book by Felix Salten

Bambi was a few days old. He loved to ask his mother questions. "Who does this path belong to?" asked Bambi.

"To us deer," answered his mother.

"What are deer?" Bambi asked.

"You are a deer," his mother laughed. "I am a deer. We are both deer. Do you understand?"

"Yes, I understand. I am a little deer, and you are a big deer!" They came to a sunny, open space.

"What is it?" asked Bambi.

"It is the meadow," answered his mother.

Literature: classic fiction

The meadow was full of new things.

"Look, mother! There's a flower flying!"

"That's not a flower. That's a butterfly."

Bambi crept closer. "Please sit still," he said to the butterfly.

"Why should I sit still?" the butterfly said. "I am a butterfly!"

"Oh, please. I want to see you up close."

"All right," said the butterfly, "but not for long."

"How beautiful you are! Like a flower!"

"Like a flower!" the butterfly cried. "I am <u>much</u> more beautiful than a flower."

"Oh, yes. Excuse me," said Bambi. "Of course you are. And you can fly. Flowers can't fly."

"Now I'm going," the butterfly said. He spread his wings and flew away.

Literature: classic fiction

Here and There

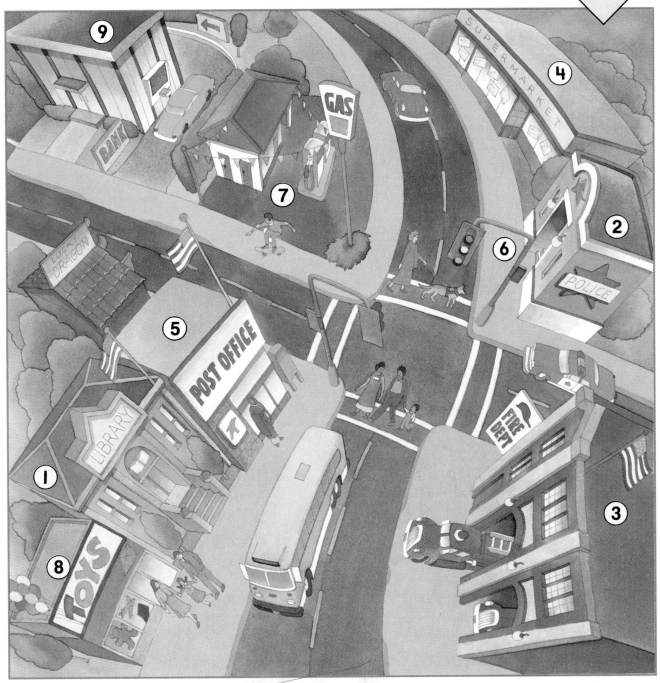

1. library	4. supermarket	7. gas station
2. police station	5. post office	8. toy store
3. fire station	6. traffic light	9. bank

 Identifying community places
Identifying location
Music: folk song

1. supermarket

2. post office

3. hardware store

4. park

5. mall

6. bank

Asking for/giving information
Role-playing fixed and free dialogues

The Weekend

Playing on the weekend, playing with my friends.
Playing on the weekend, hope it never ends.
Playing on the weekend, morning, noon or night—
Monday, it is gone.
Tuesday, it is gone.
Wednesday, it is gone.
Thursday, it is gone.
Friday, it is gone.
Monday, Tuesday, Wednesday, Thursday,
    Friday, they're all gone, and
It's the weekend!

Do you love the weekend? Why?
What do you do on the weekend?

Music: days of the week
Rhythm and rhyme
Creative writing

When I got home last night, here's what was happening.

Describing past ongoing actions
Personal story-telling

Karen was at the beach last Saturday. She was swimming and playing in the ocean. Her father was reading a book. Her mother was playing with the dog. Her baby brother was sleeping.

Sam was at the park last Sunday. He was running on the bike path. His friend was riding his bike. A man was selling hot dogs. A woman was painting a picture.

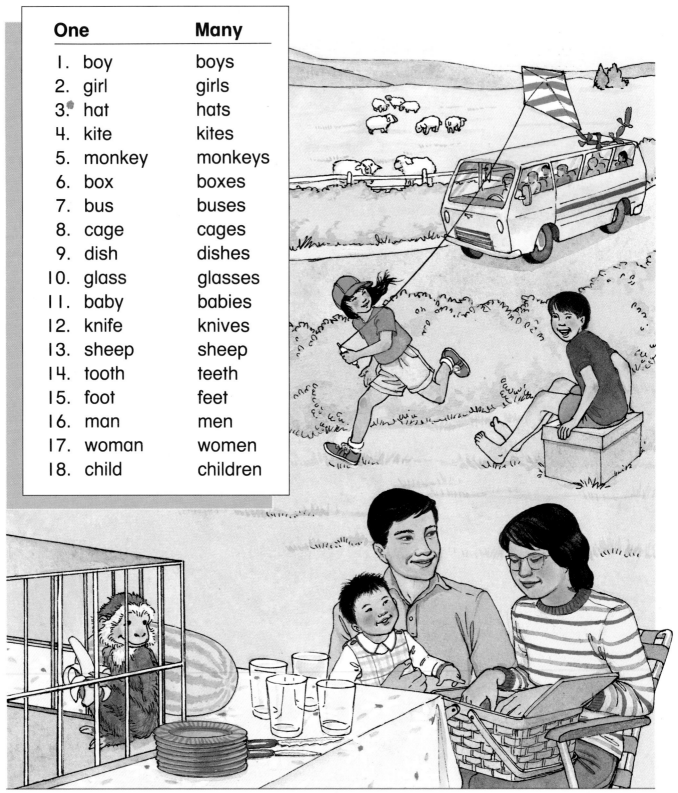

One	Many
1. boy	boys
2. girl	girls
3. hat	hats
4. kite	kites
5. monkey	monkeys
6. box	boxes
7. bus	buses
8. cage	cages
9. dish	dishes
10. glass	glasses
11. baby	babies
12. knife	knives
13. sheep	sheep
14. tooth	teeth
15. foot	feet
16. man	men
17. woman	women
18. child	children

Work with your partner.
Take turns telling how many you see.

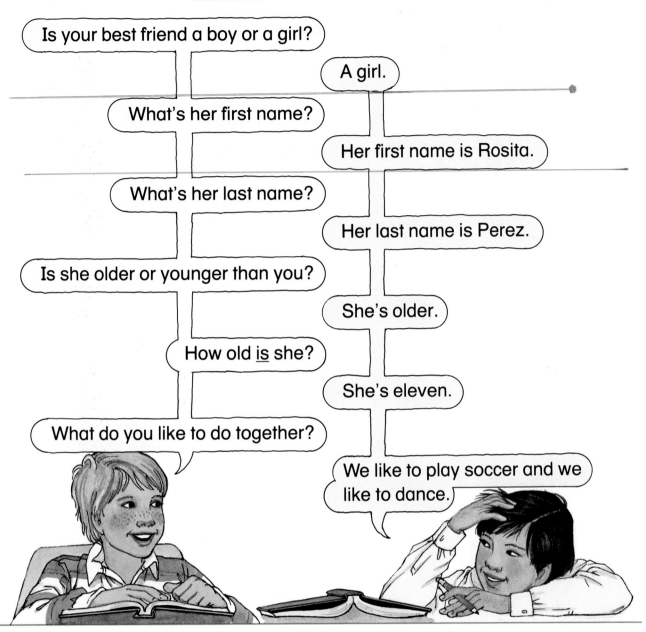

Is your best friend a boy or a girl?

A girl.

What's her first name?

Her first name is Rosita.

What's her last name?

Her last name is Perez.

Is she older or younger than you?

She's older.

How old *is* she?

She's eleven.

What do you like to do together?

We like to play soccer and we like to dance.

Make conversations about these people.

1. Bob Parker is thirteen.
   He's younger than you.
   You listen to tapes and
   play basketball together.

2. Alice Green is ten.
   She's older than you.
   You roller-skate and
   collect postcards together.

Now talk about your own best friend.

Role-playing fixed and free dialogues
Creating new dialogues from cues
Talking about self; Music

Listening Comprehension

Listen carefully. Choose the best picture.

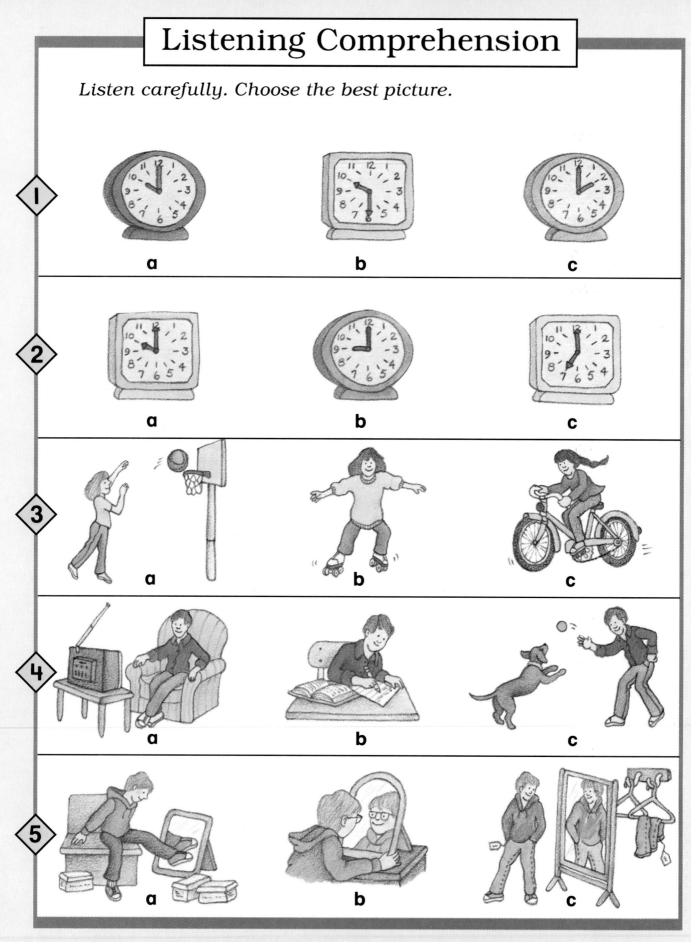

Listening Progress Check
Matching spoken language to pictures

Reading Comprehension

Read the sentence. Choose the best picture.

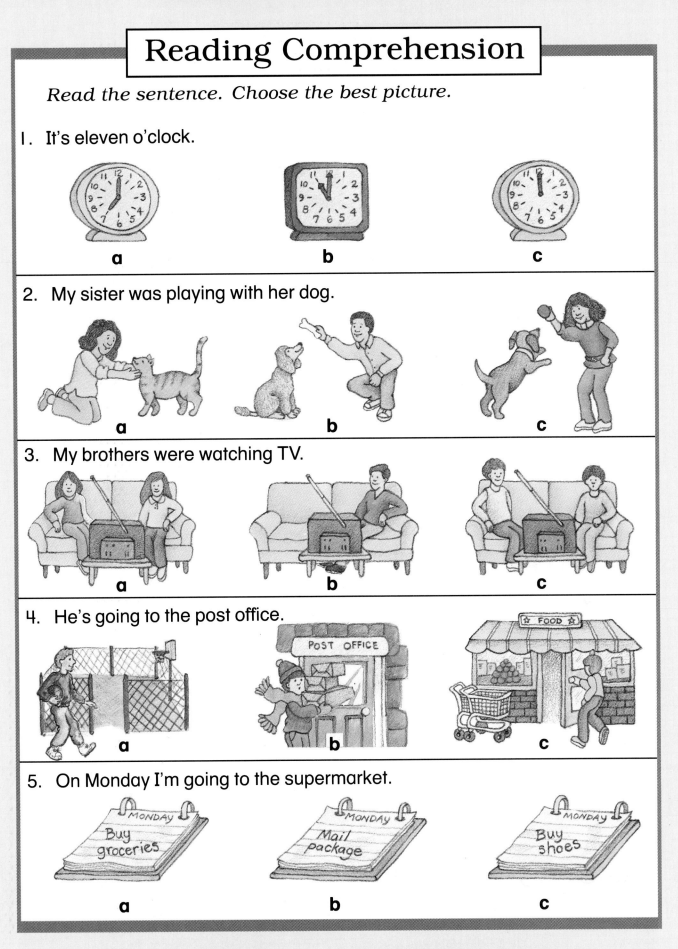

1. It's eleven o'clock.

   a   b   c

2. My sister was playing with her dog.

   a   b   c

3. My brothers were watching TV.

   a   b   c

4. He's going to the post office.

   a   b   c

5. On Monday I'm going to the supermarket.

   a   b   c

Life Skills

Role-playing fixed and free dialogues
Numbers/number words 20–100
Getting along in the community (shopping)

Say the right thing!

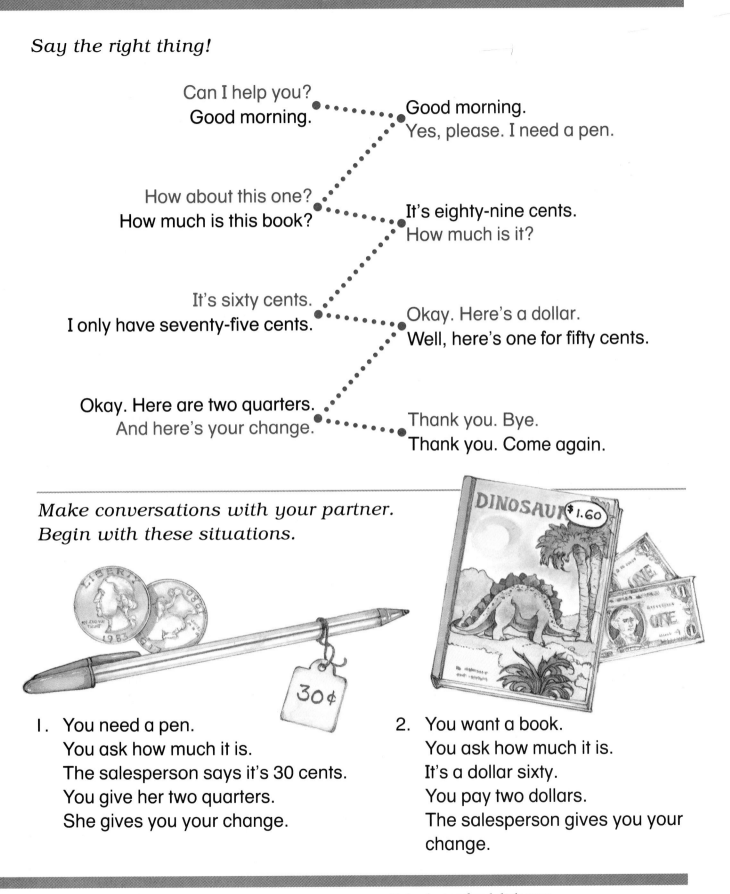

Can I help you?
Good morning.

Good morning.
Yes, please. I need a pen.

How about this one?
How much is this book?

It's eighty-nine cents.
How much is it?

It's sixty cents.
I only have seventy-five cents.

Okay. Here's a dollar.
Well, here's one for fifty cents.

Okay. Here are two quarters.
And here's your change.

Thank you. Bye.
Thank you. Come again.

Make conversations with your partner.
Begin with these situations.

DINOSAUR $1.60

30¢

1. You need a pen.
   You ask how much it is.
   The salesperson says it's 30 cents.
   You give her two quarters.
   She gives you your change.

2. You want a book.
   You ask how much it is.
   It's a dollar sixty.
   You pay two dollars.
   The salesperson gives you your change.

Role-playing fixed dialogues
Understanding sequence in conversations
Creating new dialogues from cues

55

Different Places, Different Houses

People live in many parts of the world. They live in many different climates. Some people live in a climate that is hot and dry. Other people live in a hot, rainy climate. Many people live in a climate that is cold in some months and warm in other months. What is the climate like where you live?

People make their living in different ways. Some people grow food. Some people raise animals. Some people work in offices and factories. Some people sell things in stores. How do people in your community make their living?

People live in many kinds of houses. Look at the pictures. What sort of climate do you think these people live in? What do you think their houses are made of?

Houses

There are houses
Made of wood,
And houses made of sticks;
There are houses
Made of mud,
And houses made of bricks.

There are houses
That are high,
And houses that are low;
There are houses
That are single,
And houses in a row.

There are houses
In the east,
And houses in the west;
There are houses
All around me—
But my house is the best!

Literature: poem
Rhythm and rhyme
Creative writing

CALLA: Selective attention

Liu-Always-In-A-Hurry

In China long ago, there was a farmer named Liu. He was not a patient man. He was very impatient. He was always in a hurry. He rushed through breakfast. He rushed through lunch. He rushed through his work. He wanted to be first in everything. He didn't worry about being careful in his work. He just wanted to finish it quickly.

Literature: Chinese folk tale
Shared reading
Creative writing

One day, Liu was in the village. Some farmers were talking about their rice.

"My rice is doing very well," said one farmer. "It is almost three inches high."

"My rice is already three inches high," said another farmer.

Liu hurried home. He measured his rice. The plants were strong and healthy. But they were only two inches high.

Liu decided to hurry his plants along. He pulled each plant up from the ground until it was over three inches high. "Now my rice is higher than anyone's," he thought. "Tomorrow it will be even higher!"

The next morning, Liu hurried out to his rice field. The little rice plants were dead.

The people of the village soon heard about Liu's rice. They laughed and shook their heads. They said, "Foolish Liu-always-in-a-hurry! That's what happens when you don't have any patience."

This story happened long ago. But today in China, people have a saying for someone who is not patient or careful:

Don't be a rice-puller!

Literature: Chinese folktale
Music

At Work and Play

1. doctor
2. mail carrier
3. firefighter
4. police officer
5. bus driver
6. street
7. hospital
8. bus stop
9. mailbox

1. She's a doctor.
   She helps sick people.

2. He's a chef.
   He cooks food.

3. He's a mail carrier.
   He delivers the mail.

4. She's a farmer.
   She grows corn.

5. She's a writer.
   She writes books.

6. He's a truck driver.
   He drives a truck.

Identifying occupations
Matching written language to pictures
Music: creating original verses

Does he cook meat? .... No, he doesn't.

What <u>does</u> he cook? .... He cooks fish.

Does she grow corn? .... No, she doesn't.

What <u>does</u> she grow? .... She grows flowers.

1. Does he drive a bus?

2. Does she help sick animals?

MEET THE AUTHOR

3. Does he deliver pizza?

4. Does she write letters?

Asking for/giving information
Describing habitual actions

1. He works in a restaurant.
   After work, he likes to play hockey.
   He has his skates and a helmet.

2. She works in a bank.
   After work, she likes to jog.
   She has her running shoes
   and a towel.

3. He works in a library.
   After work, he likes to paint.
   He has his brushes and paints.

4. She works in a gas station.
   After work, she likes to dance.
   She has her tapes and a tape recorder.

5. He works in a factory.
   After work, he likes to play baseball.
   He has his glove and a baseball.

Identifying leisure activities
Matching written language to pictures

Does he have a baseball? .... No, he doesn't.

What <u>does</u> he have? .... He has a helmet.

Does she have skates? .... No, she doesn't.

What <u>does</u> she have? .... She has tapes.

1. Does she have a book?

2. Does he have running shoes?

3. Does she have skates?

4. Does he have a tape recorder?

Ben is late. He brushes his teeth and washes his face in a hurry. He dresses quickly. He rushes to the bus stop. He misses the bus. He chases the bus down the street. He catches the bus at the next stop. He dashes into his office, but the office is empty! Oh no! It's Saturday! Poor Ben. He wishes he was back in bed.

How do you think Ben feels?
a. happy
b. scared
c. unhappy

Shared reading (grammar in context)
Sequencing/inferring feelings

Does he wash his hands? .... No, he doesn't.

What <u>does</u> he wash? ....He washes his face.

Does she miss the train? .... No, she doesn't.

What <u>does</u> she miss? .... She misses the bus.

1. Does he rush to the bank?

2. Does she catch a train?

3. Does he brush his hair?

4. Does she dash to the park?

I belong to a Pen Pal Club. It's lots of fun. My friends and I write to kids in other countries. They write back to us. We save the stamps from their letters. We collect them in a book. We go to the post office to buy special stamps for <u>our</u> letters. We like the stamps we get from our pals overseas.

Here are some stamps from our book. Do you know where they are from?

What is the story mostly about?
a. the post office
b. kids in other countries
c. a pen pal club

Shared reading (grammar in context)
Main idea

Pair Practice

What are you interested in?

I'm interested in music.

Do you listen to records?

No, I listen to tapes.

Do you have any other hobbies?

Yes, I collect stamps.

What do you want to be when you grow up?

I want to be a doctor.

Make conversations about these people.

1. Karen is interested in painting.
   She paints animals.
   She collects dolls.
   She wants to be a pilot.

2. Aki is interested in sports.
   He plays baseball.
   He collects baseball cards.
   He wants to be a teacher.

Now talk about yourself.

Role-playing fixed and free dialogues
Creating new dialogues from cues
Talking about self

71

Listening Comprehension

Listen carefully. Choose the best picture.

1. a   b   c
2. a   b   c
3. a   b   c
4. a   b   c
5. a   b   c

Listening Progress Check
Matching spoken language to pictures

Reading Comprehension

Look at the picture. Choose the best sentence.

1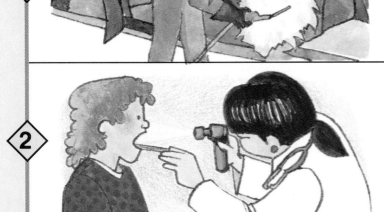
- a. He works in a factory.
- b. He works in an office.
- c. He works in a restaurant.

2
- a. She's a writer.
- b. She works in a bank.
- c. She helps sick people.

3
- a. He collects baseball cards.
- b. He likes to play hockey.
- c. He has a baseball and a glove.

4
- a. She wants to be a farmer.
- b. She wants to be a pilot.
- c. She wants to be a teacher.

5
- a. He brushes his teeth.
- b. He has glasses.
- c. He likes to brush his dog.

Life Skills

Role-playing fixed and free dialogues
Getting along in the community (library)

Say the right thing!

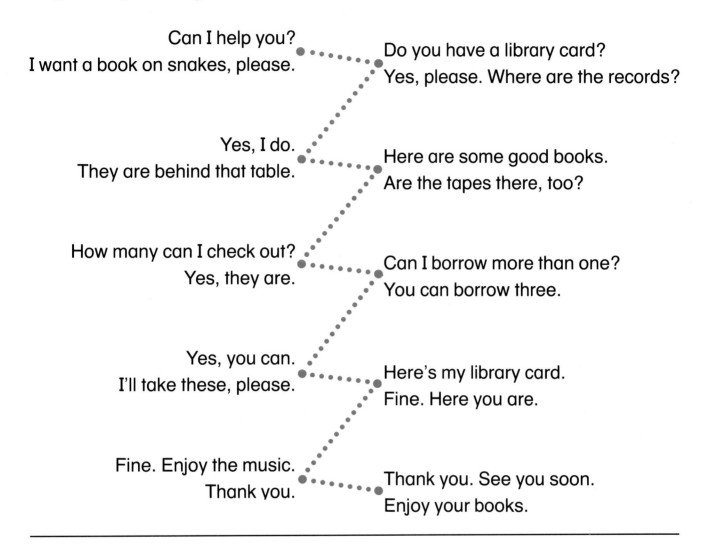

Can I help you?
I want a book on snakes, please.

Do you have a library card?
Yes, please. Where are the records?

Yes, I do.
They are behind that table.

Here are some good books.
Are the tapes there, too?

How many can I check out?
Yes, they are.

Can I borrow more than one?
You can borrow three.

Yes, you can.
I'll take these, please.

Here's my library card.
Fine. Here you are.

Fine. Enjoy the music.
Thank you.

Thank you. See you soon.
Enjoy your books.

Make conversations with your partner.
Begin with these situations.

1. You ask the librarian for a video.
   He tells you where the videos are.
   You check out two videos.
   The librarian gives you back
   your card.
   You say thank you and good-bye.

2. You're interested in books on
   sports.
   The librarian asks if you have
   a card.
   You say yes.
   You choose three books.
   The librarian hopes you'll
   enjoy them.

Role-playing fixed dialogues
Understanding sequence in conversations
Creating new dialogues from cues
75

Problem Solving

1. Anna collects stamps.
   She had 2 big stamps.
   She has 4 little stamps.
   How many stamps does Anna
   have in all?

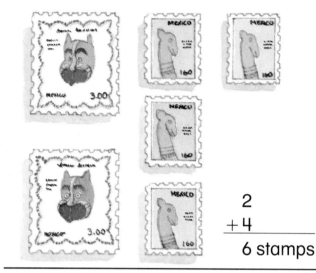

$$
\begin{array}{r}
2 \\
+\,4 \\
\hline
6 \text{ stamps}
\end{array}
$$

2. Joe collects hats.
   Tell the math story.

3. Ben collects stickers.
   Tell the math story.

4. Lisa collects shells.
   Tell the math story.

Reading a Map

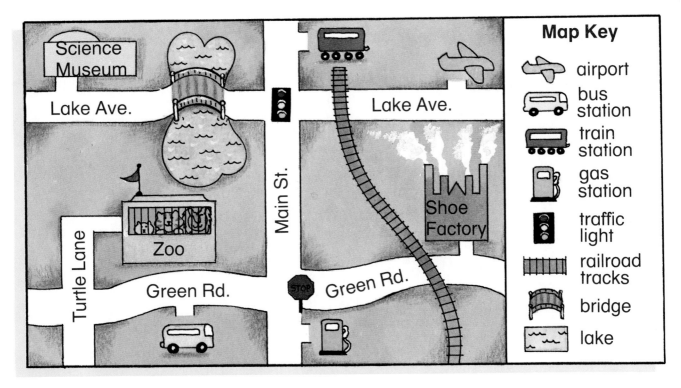

Role-play with your partner.

One of you works at the gas station.
One of you asks for directions like this:

★ Excuse me. How do I get to the **bus station?**

• Go **to the stop sign.**
  Turn left on Green Road.
  The **bus station** is on your **left.**

★ Thank you!

Use some of these words.

Turn left.	Go straight.	Go over the bridge.
Turn right.	Go to the traffic light.	Go over the railroad tracks.

The Spaceship

I dreamed I built a spaceship
Just big enough for me;
I flew around the planets,
To see what I could see.

I set my course for Saturn,
And zoomed around its rings;
I landed on a moonbeam,
And got some rocks and things.

I said hello to Venus,
And flashed around the sun;
I floated in my spacesuit,
It was a lot of fun.

I rested in the Milky Way,
And had myself a snack;
I waved to planet Jupiter,
And then I came right back!

Sophie Tyler

Literature: poem
Rhythm and rhyme
Creative writing

The Wizard of Oz

Adapted from the story by L. Frank Baum

Dorothy lived in Kansas. One day, a cyclone carried her house far, far up in the sky. Her house finally landed in the Land of Oz. It also landed right on the Wicked Witch of the East.

Strange little people called Munchkins greeted Dorothy. Their friend, the Good Witch of the North, was also there.

"Welcome! We are so grateful. You have killed the Wicked Witch of the East," said the Good Witch.

"There must be some mistake. I have not killed anything."

"Your house did, anyway. See? These are her toes!"

"But where am I?"

"In the Land of Oz, of course."

"Oh dear. Can you help me find my way back to Kansas?"

The Munchkins and the Good Witch told Dorothy to ask the Wizard of Oz for help. The Wizard lived in the City of Emeralds.

"Follow the yellow brick road," they said. "You can't miss it."

So Dorothy and her little dog Toto started along the yellow brick road. Soon, Dorothy saw a Scarecrow.

Literature: classic fiction

"Good day," said the Scarecrow. "Who are you and where are you going?"

"My name is Dorothy, and I am going to the Emerald City. I'm going to ask the great Oz to send me back to Kansas."

"Where is Emerald City, and who is Oz?"

"Don't you know?"

"No, indeed," the Scarecrow answered sadly. "I don't know anything. I have no brains at all. Do you think if I go to the Emerald City with you . . . do you think Oz would give me some brains?"

"I don't know," said Dorothy. "But you may come with me if you like. I'll ask Oz to do all he can for you."

"Thank you," said the Scarecrow.

Dorothy helped the Scarecrow over the fence and they started along the yellow brick road to the Emerald City. They had many adventures on the way. Do you know some of them?

Literature: classic fiction

Coast to Coast

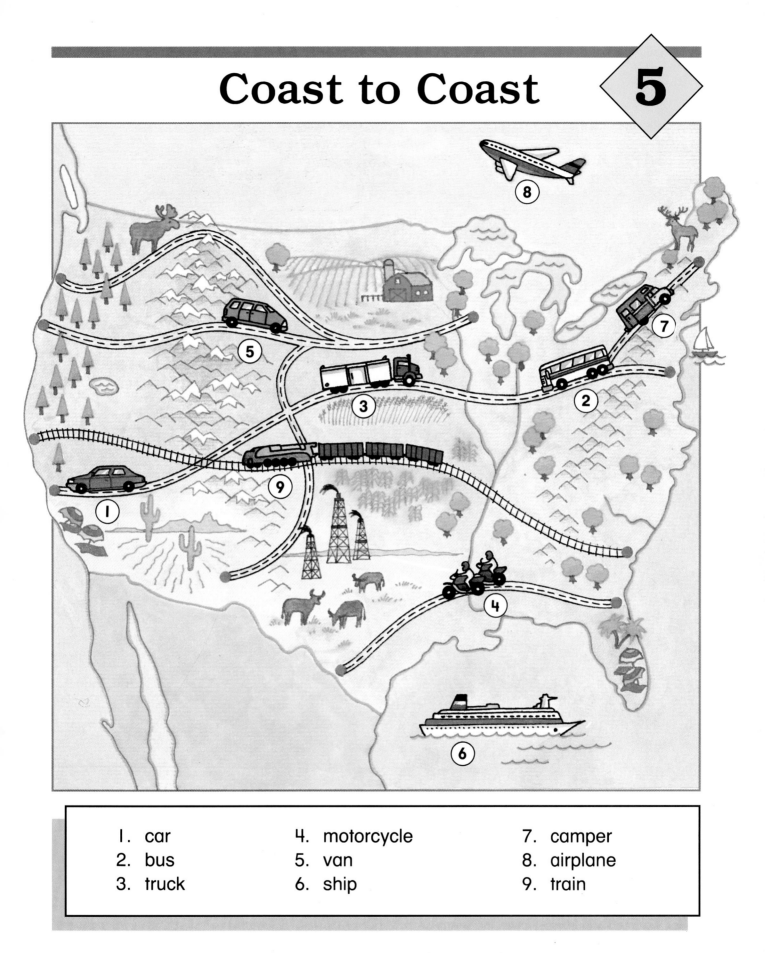

1. car	4. motorcycle	7. camper
2. bus	5. van	8. airplane
3. truck	6. ship	9. train

 Asking for/giving information
Social studies: U.S. geography/transportation

83

Did he wash his bike?............... No, he didn't.

What <u>did</u> he wash?.......... He washed his truck.

Did she lock her house?.......... No, she didn't.

What <u>did</u> she lock?.......... She locked her car.

1. What did they miss?

2. What did he cross?

3. What did she fix?

4. What did he brush?

Asking for/giving information
Describing past actions
Learning past tense ending sounds

Last night, my dad rushed home from work. He kissed my mom and said, "You rest. I'll cook dinner. I'll call you when dinner is ready," he promised. I helped him.

He fixed chicken and rice. I washed the lettuce for the salad. He sliced tomatoes and cucumbers. I tossed the salad. I mixed some pudding, too.

Finally, my father said, "Dinner is ready. Come and get it!" Everything looked really good. And you know what? It <u>was</u> good!

What did dad do first?
a. He kissed my mom.
b. He rushed home.
c. He fixed chicken and rice.

Reading (grammar in context)
Sequencing/main idea
Learning past tense ending sounds

85

Did she listen to a record?......No, she didn't.

What <u>did</u> she listen to?.....She listened to the radio.

Did he climb a ladder?..........No, he didn't.

What <u>did</u> he climb?..........He climbed a mountain.

1. What did they move?

2. What did she open?

3. What did he close?

4. What did they follow?

Asking for/giving information
Learning past tense ending sounds

I dreamed I was a rock star. I lived a great life. I traveled across the country. I stayed in the best hotels. I played my guitar for huge crowds. My fans loved me. They cheered and whistled. They listened to my records. They played my video tapes. I was famous!

What is the story mostly about?

a. Fans played his video tapes.

b. He dreamed he was a rock star.

c. Fans listened to his records.

 Reading (grammar in context)
Main idea
Music

Did he collect records?..... ....No, he didn't.

What <u>did</u> he collect?....... ......He collected stamps.

Did she paint a table?..... ....No, she didn't.

What <u>did</u> she paint?....... ....She painted a chair.

1. What did they lift?

2. What did she plant?

3. What did he want?

4. What did they count?

Asking for/giving information
Learning past tense ending sounds

She planted some seeds. She weeded the garden. She waited for the corn to grow. She sorted the good corn from the bad corn. She loaded her truck. She painted a sign. She waited for customers. She counted out ears of corn. She collected her money.

What did she do first?
a. She waited for the corn to grow.
b. She painted a sign.
c. She planted some seeds.

I am looking for my hat.
You are looking for your dog.
He is looking for his bat.
She is looking for her skate.

It is looking for its bone.
We are looking for our shoes.
You are looking for your socks.
They are looking for their sweaters.

Identifying possessions
Identifying location
Describing ongoing actions

Pair Practice

What's your favorite color? — Blue.

What's your favorite toy? — A robot.

What's your favorite food? — Ice cream.

What's your favorite school subject? — Math.

What's your favorite holiday? — July 4th.

What's your favorite hobby? — Reading.

Make conversations about these people.

1. Kelly's favorites:

red	English
bike	Christmas
carrots	playing the piano

2. Paco's favorites:

green	science
computer game	Thanksgiving
apples	watching football

Now talk about yourself.

 Role-playing fixed and free dialogues
Creating new dialogues from cues
Talking about self

91

Listen carefully. Choose the best picture.

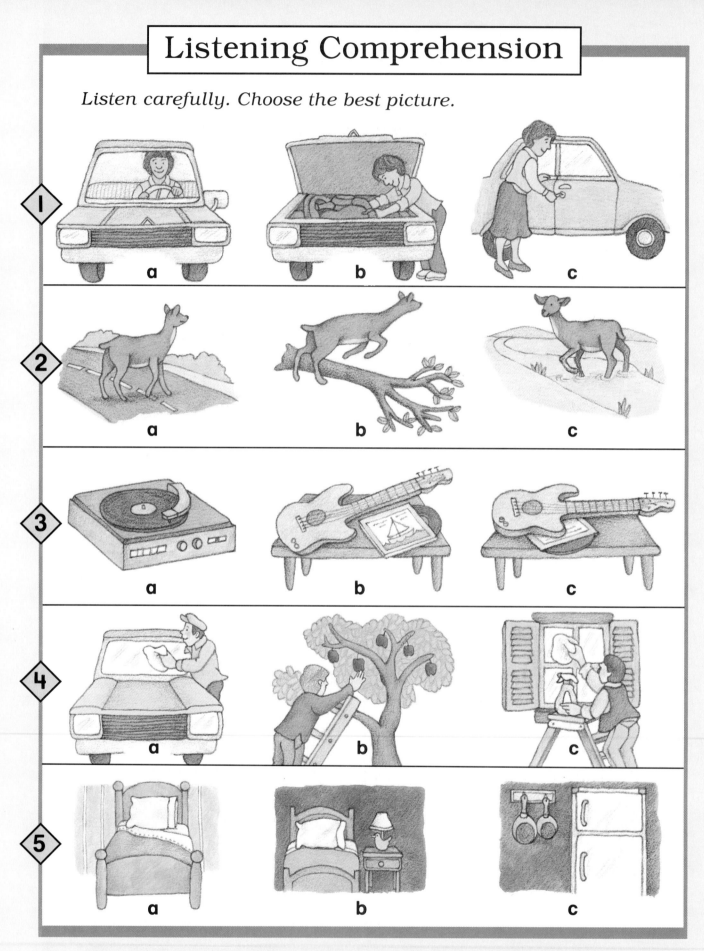

Listening Progress Check
Matching spoken language to pictures

Reading Comprehension

Read the story.
Then read the questions below the story.
Choose the best answers.

Last weekend, my family traveled to Lake George. We stayed in our camper. On Saturday, we climbed a mountain. On Sunday, we played by the lake. It was a wonderful weekend.

1. Where did the family stay?
    a. in a big hotel
    b. in a little hotel
    c. in their camper

2. What did the family do on Sunday?
    a. They climbed a mountain.
    b. They played by the lake.
    c. They stayed in bed.

3. What is this story mostly about?
    a. a trip to Lake George
    b. a little hotel
    c. my family

Yesterday was Thanksgiving. Sam's family cooked a big dinner. The dinner was good! After dinner, Sam turned on the TV. The family watched the football game. It was lots of fun.

4. What did the family do first?
    a. They cooked dinner.
    b. They watched a football game.
    c. They turned on the TV.

5. How did the family feel about their holiday?
    a. They were happy.
    b. They were sad.
    c. They were angry.

6. What is this story mostly about?
    a. a football game
    b. a nice Thanksgiving
    c. a big dinner

Reading Progress Check
Identifying details/sequencing
Inferring feelings/main idea

93

Life Skills

Role-playing fixed and free dialogues

Say the right thing!

Good morning. How are you?
Hi. How are you doing?

Fine, thanks. How about you?
Not so good.

Just okay. I still have a cold.
What's the matter?

Well, I hope you feel better soon.
I have a bad cold.

That's too bad. Well, get better.
Thanks. So do I.

See you later.
I'll try.

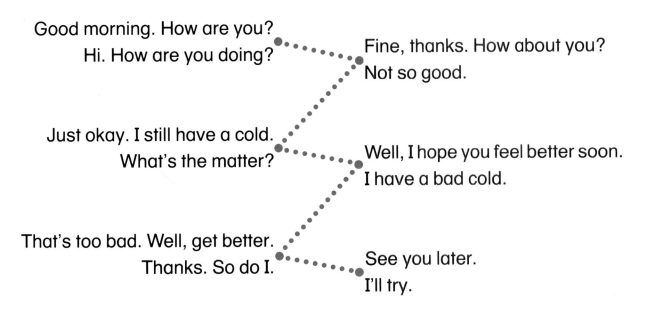

Make conversations with your partner.
Begin with these situations.

1. Your friend doesn't come to school.
   You call your friend.
   Your friend has a cold.
   You hope your friend will be better soon.

2. You wake up feeling sick.
   Your mom asks you what's the matter.
   You have a stomachache.
   Your mom says she's sorry.

Role-playing fixed dialogues
Understanding sequence in conversations
Creating new dialogues from cues

95

Light and Shadows

Stand in the sun.
Have your friend measure your shadow.
Do this three times:

early in the morning
at lunchtime
late in the afternoon

Make a graph. Your teacher will help you.

My Shadow

Time of Day	1ft	2ft	3ft	4ft	5ft	6ft	7ft	8ft	9ft	10ft
Early morning	▨	▨	▨	▨	▨	▨	▨	▨	▨	
Lunchtime	▨	▨	▨							
Late afternoon	▨	▨	▨	▨	▨	▨	▨			

Science: solar motion, shadows
Graphing
Expressing comparisons

Try this experiment.

Shine light on the pins.
Find the shadow on the cardboard.
Move the light.
Make all the shadows fall in the same direction.

Make all the shadows fall outside the circle.
Do the shadows fall toward the light source
or away from it?

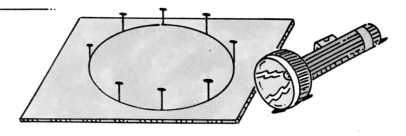

Where was the sun when this picture was taken?
How do you know?

The Elephant Carries a Great Big Trunk

The elephant carries a great big trunk;
He never packs it with clothes;
It has no lock, and it has no key,
But he takes it wherever he goes!

Way Down South

Way down South where bananas grow,
A grasshopper stepped on an elephant's toe.
The elephant said, with tears in his eyes,
"Pick on somebody your own size."

Literature: poems
Rhythm and rhyme
Creative writing

The Little Ant

It was March. The little ant looked outside.
"Mama," she said. "It is spring! May I play outside?"

"No," her mother answered. "Spring has not come
yet. It is still too cold for a little ant to play outside."

But Little Ant didn't listen. She ran outside. But
soon, she felt cold. And it began to snow.

"Mama was right," she thought. "I'm going home
right now."

But just then, a big snowflake landed on her. And
a big leaf landed on the snowflake. Little Ant couldn't
move!

Literature: Hispanic tale
Shared reading/sequencing/predicting
Role-playing

Little Ant called to *La Nieve,* the snow:

"Snow, let go, so I can go home!"

But the snow wouldn't let go.

Little Ant called to *La Hoja,* the leaf:

"Leaf, fly away with the snow;
Snow, let go, so I can go home!"

But the leaf wouldn't fly away.

Little Ant called to *El Raton,* the mouse:

"Mouse, lift the leaf;
Leaf, fly away with the snow;
Snow, let go, so I can go home!"

But the mouse wouldn't lift the leaf.

Little Ant called to *El Gato,* the cat:

"Cat, catch the mouse;
Mouse, lift the leaf;
Leaf, fly away with the snow;
Snow, let go, so I can go HOME!"

But the cat wouldn't chase the mouse.

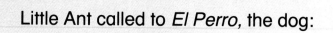

Little Ant called to *El Perro,* the dog:

"Dog, chase the cat;
Cat, catch the mouse;
Mouse, lift the leaf;
Leaf, fly away with the snow;
Snow, let GO, so I can GO HOME!"

But the dog wouldn't chase the cat.

Literature: Hispanic tale

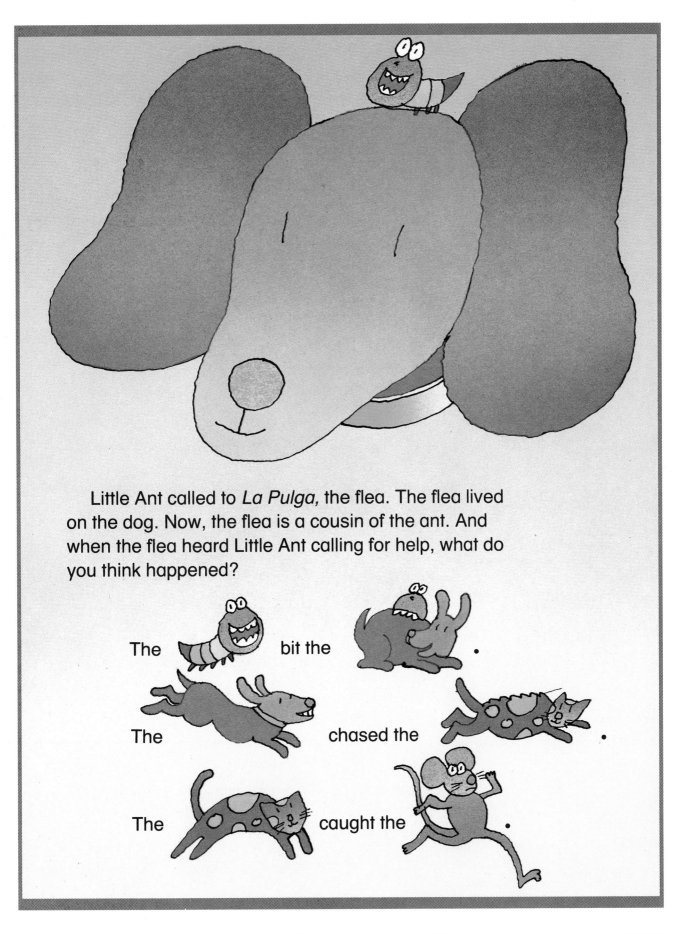

Little Ant called to *La Pulga,* the flea. The flea lived on the dog. Now, the flea is a cousin of the ant. And when the flea heard Little Ant calling for help, what do you think happened?

The [flea] bit the [dog] .

The [dog] chased the [cat] .

The [cat] caught the [mouse] .

The lifted the .

The flew away with the and

The FINALLY let go of the .

Little Ant ran straight home. And she didn't go out to play again. . . not until her mother said spring had come for sure!

Literature: Hispanic tale
Music

Through the Year

6

Spring

Summer

Fall

Winter

1. seeds	3. hose	5. broom
2. plants	4. rake	6. shovel

Identifying/describing
Sequencing
Music: folk song

105

In the spring, they have to work.
She has to dig up the ground.
He has to plant the seeds.

In the summer, they
have to work.
She has to pull up the weeds.
He has to water the plants.

In the fall, they have to work.
She has to rake the leaves.
He has to sweep the walk.

In the winter, they have to work.
She has to scrape off the car.
He has to shovel the walk.

After they work, they enjoy their yard.
What do you think they do?

Describing actions
     Sequencing

1. go to the dentist

2. deliver papers

3. practice my piano lessons

4. watch my baby sister

5. clean my room

6. go shopping

1. When did he get up? .... He got up at nine.

2. What did he eat? .... He ate some eggs.

3. What did he drink? .... He drank some juice.

4. Where did he go? .... He went to the river.

5. What did he ride? .... He rode a motorcycle.

6. What did he catch? .... He caught a fish.

Asking for/giving information
Describing past actions
Learning irregular past tense

Kim got up early. She took a shower and got dressed. She ate some cereal and drank some milk.

She got on her bike. She went to the corner. She put twenty newspapers in her basket. She rode through the neighborhood. She delivered all the papers. Then she caught the bus for school.

What is the story mostly about?
a. Kim got up early.
b. Kim had a busy morning.
c. Kim got on her bike.

 Shared reading (grammar in context)
Sequencing/main idea
109

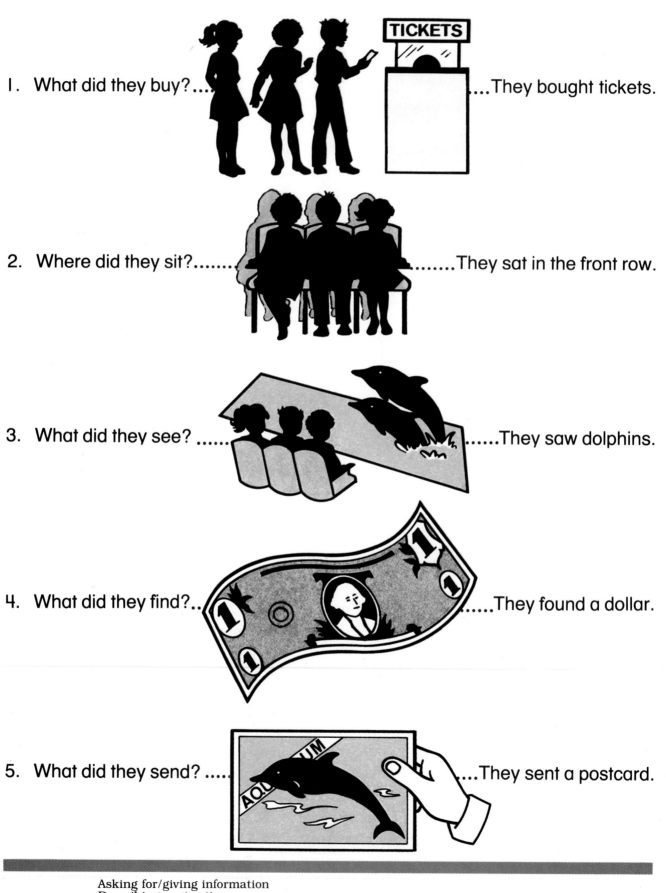

1. What did they buy?....................They bought tickets.

2. Where did they sit?.....................They sat in the front row.

3. What did they see? ....They saw dolphins.

4. What did they find?....................They found a dollar.

5. What did they send? ....They sent a postcard.

Asking for/giving information
Describing past actions
Learning irregular past tense

It was my mom's birthday last Saturday. On Wednesday, my brother and I went shopping. We found a pretty scarf. We bought it and wrapped it in red paper.

On Saturday morning, my grandmother and I made a cake. I wrote Happy Birthday on it. We put one big candle in the middle.

On Saturday night, we had a party. We sang "Happy Birthday," and my mom blew out the candle. She opened her presents and cards. She got a lot of nice presents. But she said she liked the scarf best of all.

How did mom feel on Saturday?
a. sad and tired
b. surprised and happy
c. tired and scared

Shared reading (grammar in context)
Sequencing/main idea
Inferring feelings

111

1. It's a quarter after one.
    It's one fifteen.

2. It's half past one.
    It's one thirty.

3. It's a quarter to two.
    It's one forty-five.

4. It's two o'clock.

5.   6.   7.   8.

Make conversations with your partner like this:

★ Let's go to the **movies** on **Saturday.**

● Okay. What time do you want to go?

★ At **two thirty.**

Telling time (half past, quarter to/after)
Role-playing fixed and free dialogues
Describing planned future actions

Pair Practice

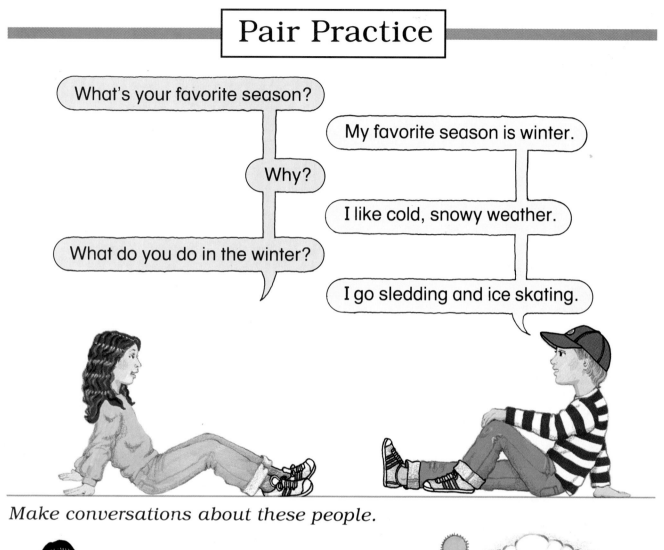

What's your favorite season?

My favorite season is winter.

Why?

I like cold, snowy weather.

What do you do in the winter?

I go sledding and ice skating.

Make conversations about these people.

 My favorite season is summer.
I like hot, sunny weather.
I go swimming and sailing.

 My favorite season is fall.
I like cool, windy weather.
I go bike riding. I play in the leaves.

 My favorite season is spring.
I like warm, rainy days.
I plant flowers in my yard.

Now talk about yourself.

 Role-playing fixed and free dialogues
Creating new dialogues from cues
Talking about self

113

Listening Comprehension

Listen carefully. Choose the best picture.

Listening Progress Check
Matching spoken language to pictures

Reading Comprehension

Read the story.
Then read the questions below the story.
Choose the best answers.

Yesterday morning Jeff got up early. He wanted to surprise his mother. He went into the kitchen. He made some coffee. He sliced a banana. He put juice, milk, and cereal on the table. Then he went to his mother's room.

"Good morning, Mom," he said. "Come to the kitchen. There's something special for you!"

It was October. Julie and Carmen were in school. They looked out the window. The leaves on the trees were red, yellow, and brown.

"This is my favorite season," Julie said to her friend.

"It's not my favorite season," said Carmen. "I like summer best."

1. What did Jeff do first?
   a. He made coffee.
   b. He put juice on the table.
   c. He went to his mother's room.

2. How do you think his mother felt when she came to the kitchen?
   a. surprised and scared
   b. surprised and angry
   c. surprised and happy

3. What do you think Jeff and his mother did next?
   a. They went shopping.
   b. They ate breakfast.
   c. They delivered newspapers.

4. Where were Julie and Carmen?
   a. at home
   b. in school
   c. under a tree

5. Who is Carmen?
   a. Julie's teacher
   b. Julie's sister
   c. Julie's friend

6. What is Julie's favorite season?
   a. spring
   b. fall
   c. winter

Role-playing fixed and free dialogues
Ordinals
Getting along in the community (taking a bus)

Say the right thing!

Fares, please.
You stop at the park, don't you?

Can you change a dollar?
Yes, I do.

Sorry. Exact fare only.
How many stops is it?

It's two stops.
Here you are. How far is it to the bank?

You're on the wrong bus.
So I get off at the third stop?

What? You don't go to the bank?
No, you get off at the second stop.

No, I don't. You want bus 58.
Thank you.

You're welcome.
Thank you.

Make conversations with your partner.

1. You are on the bus.
    You ask for the library.
    You're on the wrong bus.
    You want bus number 33.

2. You are on the bus.
    You ask for the post office.
    It's the third stop.
    You pay your fare.

Role-playing fixed dialogues
Understanding sequence in conversations
Creating new conversations from cues

117

Problem Solving

1. Jenny had

Jenny had 80 cents.
She bought a postcard.   80¢
The postcard cost 40 cents. − 40¢
How much money was left?   40¢

2. Ramon had

Tell the math story.

3. Laura had

Tell the math story.

4. George had

Tell the math story.

Reading a Map

There are 50 states in the United States of America. Ohio is one of the 50 states. A state has many cities and towns in it.

One city in each state is called the capital of the state. The laws of the state are made in the capital.

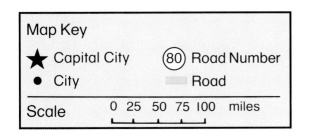

Map Key

★ Capital City ⑧⓪ Road Number
● City ▬ Road

Scale   0 25 50 75 100   miles

Work with your partner. Look at the map of Ohio.
Use it to answer these questions.

1. What is the capital of Ohio?
   (Use the map key.)
2. Name a state that is west of Ohio.
3. Name a state that is east of Ohio.
4. About how far is it from Cincinnati
   to Cleveland? (Use the scale of miles.)
5. What is north of Cleveland?
6. You are going from Dayton to Cincinnati.
   What is the number of the road you take?
   What direction do you travel on this road?

With your partner, ask and answer other questions
about the map of Ohio. Use some of these words.

north	east	city	lake
south	west	road	distance

Dreams

Hold fast to dreams
For if dreams die
Life is a broken-winged bird
That cannot fly.

Hold fast to dreams
For when dreams go
Life is a barren field
Frozen with snow.

Langston Hughes

Literature: poem
Rhythm and rhyme
Creative writing

The Grateful Statues

Long ago in Japan, a poor man and his wife lived in a small village. She made straw hats. Her husband sold the hats by the roadside.

One day the man said, "It's the last day of the year. We must make some rice cakes. We must celebrate the New Year tomorrow."

"But we have no rice," said the wife. "And we have no money to buy rice. What shall we do?"

He felt very sad. He and his wife could not celebrate the New Year without rice cakes. Without rice cakes, the New Year would be filled with bad fortune.

"I will sell these five hats," said the man.

"But it is so cold outside," said the woman. "Don't go."

Literature: Japanese tale

But the man went out to try to sell the hats. It was very cold. No one was out on the road. Everybody was home, making rice cakes. It started to snow. The old man decided to return home.

He came to six statues. They were statues of Jizo, the protector of children. The man thought, "The statues must be cold, even though they are made of stone."

He gave each statue a hat. He gave the sixth statue his own hat. The man was almost frozen when he got home.

He told his wife the bad news. "No one was out on the road. I gave the hats to the statues of Jizo. I gave away my hat, too."

"Don't feel so sad," his wife said. "Let's just go to bed. At least we can keep warm there."

Literature: Japanese tale

While the old couple slept, something magical happened. A song floated out of the woods.

A kind, good man,
Poor and old,
Gave us hats to save us
From the cold.

That kindness we
Will now repay,
And give him rice cakes
On New Year's Day.

What a surprise the old couple had in the morning!
Outside their door, they found two huge rice cakes.
They were the freshest, richest rice cakes they had
ever seen. Now they could celebrate the New Year.
And the year would be filled with happiness and good
fortune.

And in the distance, you could see six statues. They
were walking back to the snowy woods, protected by
their straw hats.

Literature: Japanese tale

Skills Index

For a complete inventory of skills development in this level,
see the Scope and Sequence Chart in the Teacher's Edition.

Linguistic Skills

Structures

adjectives
  comparative, superlative 96
  descriptive 26
  demonstrative 23, 28, 29
  possessive 6, 10, 11, 26, 28, 29, 90
count/non-count nouns 50
did questions 84, 86, 88, 107
do/does questions 7, 9, 27, 31, 65, 67, 69
let's + verb 112
or questions 31, 51
prepositions of place 23, 30, 43
singular/plural nouns 50
subject/object pronouns 30
there is/are 8, 43
wh- questions (throughout)

Verbs

future tense: *going to* 45
future tense: *will* 10
habitual present tense 7, 9, 11, 64-69, 106, 113
like to 9, 51, 66
modals
  can/can't 30, 44, 54
  have to/had to 106, 107
past progressive tense 48, 49
past tense, irregular 48, 108-111
past tense, regular 84-89, 107
present progressive tense 24, 25, 30, 44, 90
present tense: *to be* 7, 9, 11, 23, 26, 31, 47, 51, 54, 55, 64, 71, 91, 113
present tense: *to have* 27, 31, 66, 67, 94
want to 71, 112

Oral Communication

asking for/giving directions 4
asking for/giving information (throughout)
asking for/giving personal information 6, 10, 11, 31
asking for/giving preferences 7, 9
creating new dialogues from cues 11, 15, 31, 35, 51, 55, 71, 75, 91, 95, 113, 117
describing
  a scene 50, 83, 106

actions 63, 83, 106
cost 54, 55, 116, 117
habitual actions 64-66, 69, 70, 71, 106, 113
health 94, 95
location 23, 30, 43, 63, 90
past actions 84, 88, 107, 108
past ongoing actions 48, 49
physical characteristics 26
planned future actions 112
present ongoing actions 30, 50, 90
quantity 27, 50, 115-117
time 47, 112
expressing
  feelings 46, 68, 111
  likes 91, 113
  needs, wants, requests 34, 35, 71, 74, 75
  obligations 106, 107
  ownership 28, 29, 90
  thanks 14, 15
following conversational sequence 15, 31, 35, 72, 95, 117
identifying
  family members/relationships 23, 26, 27
  leisure activities 66
  occupations 63, 64
  places in school 4
  possessions 28, 29, 90
  things 3, 23
personal story-telling 26, 31, 48, 49
talking about self 11, 51, 71, 91, 113

Reading Skills

developing comprehension skills 19-22, 27, 36, 39-42, 49, 56, 57, 59-62, 79-82, 96, 97, 99-104, 108, 109, 117, 119-127
drawing conclusions 97
identifying the main idea 70, 78, 82, 85, 87, 89, 93, 99-104, 109, 111
inferring 57, 59-62, 93, 111, 115
learning language through poems 58, 78, 98, 120
predicting 79-82, 99-104, 115
reading a paragraph: past tense in context 85, 87, 89, 109, 111

recalling details 79-82, 93, 97, 99-104, 108, 115, 121-127
recognizing rhyme, rhythm 38, 46, 78, 98, 120
relating reading to own experience 56, 106, 121-127
retelling a story 19-22, 70, 76, 89, 90
shared reading and discussion: literature 39-42, 59-62, 79-82, 99-104, 121-127
shared reading and discussion: non-fiction 19-22, 56, 57
understanding cause and effect 59-62
using poems as models for own poems 58, 78, 98, 120

Learning in the Content Areas

Math

describing cost 54, 55
describing quantity 76
measuring size 16
measuring weight 17
ordinal numbers 116
solving word problems 76, 118

Science

charting, graphing 36, 96
classifying 97
comparing 37, 96
constructing a scale 17
drawing conclusions 97
identifying body parts 36-38
measuring shadows 96-97
solar motion 96-97

Social Studies

climate 56, 57
geography 18, 19-22, 56, 83, 119
history 18, 19-22
transportation 83
using maps 77, 119

Life Skills

asking for/giving directions 4, 77
following directions 12, 13, 16, 17, 32, 33, 52, 53, 72, 73, 92, 93, 96, 97, 114, 115, 119
getting along in the community 43, 74, 94, 116, 117
identifying money 54
telling time 47, 112